Footprints of My Mind

Footprints of My Mind

(A Collection of Poems)

Neerja Sachdev

Published in 2025 by Notionpress, India

E-mail: dr.neerjasachdev@gmail.com

Footprint of My Mind (A Collection of Poems)

Copyright © 2025 Neerja Sachdev

ISBN: 978-889588574-1

Content

Personal Poems

ABOUT THE POET

Dr. Neerja Sachdev was the youngest child of her parents and dreamt from her childhood to be a teacher in life. She always had a passion for teaching children and cherished the aura of being surrounded by her students. Her parents, Dr. L.P. Mehrotra and Mrs. Kamla Mehrotra, were both senior psychologists, who delved poignantly into the minds of the people and showered their blessing and understanding on people from all walks of life who approached them for help. She had the freedom to make her own decisions, and she sailed smoothly through the path of being an educator, a Teacher. Her wishes were never hampered and after completing her schooling from St. Mary's Convent, Allahabad, she joined the University of Allahabad completing her graduation and post-graduation in English Literature with flying colours obtaining VIth position in the merit list of her Bachelor's Degree. After passing her Master's Degree in first division she did her D. Phil. in American Literature. Her specialization was in the field of Black Women Writers.

The tides of life favoured her and she was appointed as a lecturer in English Literature in S.S. Khanna Girls' Degree

College, Allahabad in 1980 where she worked for 42 years teaching graduate and postgraduate students. She retired as an Associate Professor and Vice Principal of the college in June 2022. She was appointed as a member in multifarious committees, Chairperson of the U.G.C. Committee, Coordinator of the Commerce Faculty, Programme Officer of N.S.S. and Rovers Rangers.

She has edited two books, "Relevance of Education to life" (2016) and "*Absolute Swaraj*" (2018). She has been the co-editor of the journal "Anveeksha". She organized two National Seminars and a Workshop in her college. She has also presented papers in many National/International journals. She has received "Rashtriya Gaurav Award" by Citizen Society in 2015 and "Acti Award" by Educational Society in 2012.

She is now a bi-lingual poetess who has recently published her Anthology of Hindi poems *'Kalpanaon Ka Manthan'* in March 2024.She has published a short story and her creative bent of mind has made her an artist. Her paintings exhibit her diverse thoughts and visionary mind.

FOREWORD

The evolution of a poetry book stems from the soul of a poet, as they spill their ink from the well that resides in the core of their being. In the Poetry collection, "Footprints of My Mind," by Dr. Neerja Sachdev, this truth remains apparent and alive, for she has composed a delightful and eclectic culmination of word art in poetic form. It is quite apparent in her poetic compositions that she writes as one educated in poetic style, yet innately has gained the ability to compromise her own uniqueness, which has evolved into her own signature of writing.

The reader is able to embrace the appropriateness of the deemed title, as the writer possesses the capability to provide sage enlightenment as she broaches subject matters that only a matured mind with life's lessons and experiences could. With an eloquent feminist voice, she is able to embody the beauty that exists in the strength and courage that evolves from necessity to overcome injustices and abuse. A poetic is a phoenix, rising above the ashes to transition into the victor, denying all rights of a subsequent victim.

The author's graceful words describe the embodiment of a woman, her many duties that stem from her appointed roles as wife and mother. Not only, given the sacred ability to give birth and nurture, is the woman the epitome of love and selflessness, bearing the burdens of life as they herald on, without complaint. One's ability to juggle the burdens of life and strife, with the discovery of "finding the golden jewel of peace within." Despite having the life's turbulences, she has the capacity to relish the peace and tranquility there within.

The author speaks of the joys and burdens of memories, themselves the footprints leading us on a journey where wisdom and experience are gained, "Helps you steer the voyage of your life's ship." Methodically, she crafts the poem of "Stranger to Yourself," with a digested view of our ability to peep through the doors of our inner self, we in turn are able to feast upon that entity, thus, no longer being a stranger to yourself.

In writing of the hardships of loneliness, she divulges the solace that can be found in artistic creativity, as a means to cope with the loneliness, finding comfort and purpose. The author possesses the talents to paint metaphorical pictures of clouds, giving meaning to the obscurity they can display. Paying homage to America, while giving valid sound advice- "Stand as a stalwart to the nation, but never forget the root of your destination."

She speaks of dreams…the reality and potentiality of them. The journey of "Introspection," is our ability to analyze and scrutinize, in effort to identify our true selves. She weaves through the complexities of love that reign within the simplicity of emotion, love reigning supreme is the ebb and flow of life.

The aforementioned subject matters are only a fraction of the gift of works Dr. Neerja Sachdev has so graciously bestowed in her timeless book, *The Footprints of My Mind*. A book that is sure to be filled with bookmarks, and dog-eared pages, for reflective analysis of works written from the heart, with a sage filled mind. May her pen be contained with endless ink, and her mind filled with the constitution to further grace the reader with her timeless works. I wish her all the best for her poetry collections.

Annette (Wengert) Tarpley

Poet, Writer, Author, &

Founder of "The Passion of Poetry"

PREFACE

"Take only memories, leave only footprints" Chief Seattle's quote very aptly applies to my book of poems "Footprints of my Mind" which will surely efface its footprints on the mind of everyone.

During the span of two torrid and turbulent years of Corona, we were confined to our home but with the work from home I could snatch a few moments to pen down my thoughts in verses on different subjects. Writing crystallizes my thoughts and they are like Wordsworth's "spontaneous overflow of thoughts in tranquility." My random thoughts sometimes went haywire, but I disciplined them by putting them in verse form. My poems trace feminist thoughts on "Womanhood", "The Trials of life", 'Lost Bird", "Be a Survivor, not a Victim" to pensive "Thoughts", "Hope" "Fear", "Peace", to nature "Clouds" and abstract feeling of "Loneliness" "Solitude", "Laziness", leading to "Relationship" and "Belongingness". "Brotherhood, "Sisterhood," "Motherhood" was also touched upon, besides highlighting personal bondage with near and dear ones. I could not miss expressing my thoughts on "Corona" "Lockdown" and invigorating hope that "Bells were still Ringing during Lockdown".

Tracing the pattern of life and traversing through its narrow pathways, I opened the petals of my "Thoughts" and felt enamored by the empathy, love and closeness of my family members who stood by me always and extended their warmth and support. "My brother, my treasure" my "Loving Son", "My daughter", my dearest sisters who hold the everlasting bonds of "Sisterhood", "My Beloved", companion, friend and lover, my lovable daughter-in-law dear "Priti", my "Guru and Shishya" all stood as pillars and strength in my life, upheld my values and blessed me always.

I retired from my teaching profession in June 2022 and my confinement at home triggered my creativity in drawing portraits and maneuvering various art forms because I learnt life is not about finding yourself but life is about creating yourself through the immense magic of picking up a brush and making it flow with various colors in life. I tried to sketch a few pictures related to my poems which are a reflection of their footprints in my mind. I took this adventure of living my life of dreams by translating every thought imprinted in my mind, making it come alive on canvas because life doesn't require that we be the best only but besides being a novice in this field, I showcased what was my best. The artist in me propelled me to draw and paint my thoughts in art form outlining the interiors of the windows of my mind.

After all the privations and tribulations searching "Peace", "Tranquility", by looking into "Mirror" with self "Introspection", it enhanced me to steer the ship of my life with vigor and independence. I realized that every dream can come true with your strength, patience and passion to reach out for the zenith. My paintings are my contributions of unwavering commitment of resilience and wisdom that will continue to inspire devotees of art.

My poems are thought provoking and with the benediction of God and blessings of all of you, I sincerely wish that my book of poems shall win laurels and be cherished by all and sundry. Hope to get a positive response from the readers.

Neerja Sachdev

ACKNOWLEDGEMENT

I must acknowledge my regards and gratitude to my husband Captain Brij Mohan Sachdev who was my backbone in promoting me to write and publish my work. My heartfelt thanks to him.

While sailing through the ebb and flow of mental tides my sister, Dr. Nalini Tandon stood as a pillar of strength in my creative art of composing poems. She encouraged and strengthened me. I bow in obeisance to her for her constant support.

I feel obliged and extend my deep regards and thanks to Mr. Ghanshyam, a multitasked senior employee of my college who gave his precious time in typing my poems.

My special thanks and love to Dr. Shamenaz for inspiring me to keep writing and progressing. Her guidance and help were a blessing in disguise.

I am extremely thankful to my family, friends and children.

WOMANHOOD

W in you aspires for Wealth,

O pinpoints the organizer in you,

M promotes you as a Manager within,

A sensitizes your Amorousness hidden,

N ennobles you to Nurture herein.

Woman, I define you as a creator of mankind,

For, Darwin's theory of origin may fall behind.

You turn the Wheel of Fortune in life,

For without you, we fail to hold the threads of life.

Woman, you are the torchbearer of life.

A guide, a mentor, and a guardian, so bright.

You are the sweetheart of your lover,

A wife, a sister and a caretaker in all.

Woman, you readily transcend your past.

To live steadily in the present.

Forgetting the bitter-sweet memories,

Of childhood and adolescence in anamnesis.

Woman, you are the Knight -in-Arms.

A soldier who battles with strife.

Manipulates, caresses, and cajoles,

And wins the heart through her multifarious roles.

Woman, you are a physician at heart.

Who medicates and nurses the sick with art.

You are the medicine in disguise,

For with your healing powers, you purge without egress.

Woman, you are an Architect

Who stands as the pillar of the house.

With your courage and hardihood,

You hold the fortress with fortitude,

Woman, you are the Legislator.

Who formulates rules and governs the house.

No child can transgress nor cause traumatic rupture,

Nor trigger your rage without a vigour.

Woman, you are an artist.

Who sketches her own tree of life.

Filling in with colours of sweetness on all sides,

And painting the canvas of veritable beauty with all might.

Woman, you are the soul of mankind.

A saint, a benefactor and a devout sublime.

You forgive the sins of all dear to you,

For you are your own God alive within you.

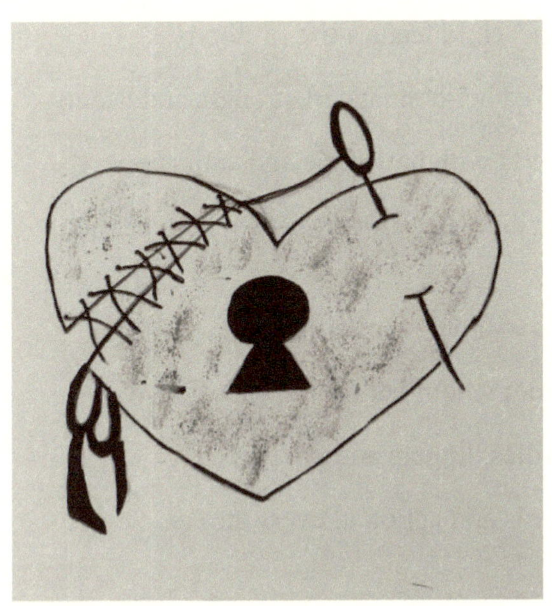

BE A SURVIVOR, NOT THE VICTIM

She was chirpy, innocent, gullible and free,

Like a bird ready with wings to fly.

Never realizing that soon they will be clipped,

Leaving scars with indelible prints.

A flower germinates and blossoms.

But if you nip its bud before it grooms,

It will die many deaths each day,

Without rejuvenating into its real self again.

Thus a budding girl child leads a life of liberty.

Marriage soon gives her bondage of strength and beauty.

She enters a new life with new hope and enthusiasm,

But very soon she digresses from this path with passion.

She did her duties without recognition.

With the man, under whom her spells were ridden.

Who dallies, dawdles, lingers and pokes,

Licensing her words and action at every stroke.

He scrutinizes her each day, with every activity.

Manoeuvring her plans with suspicion.

Hurling abuses at her family and friends.

Curbing her rights to extreme ends.

The night gets dark and the candles are all out.

She stood trembling, helpless without support.

He groped at her, with hands clutched at each part

Of her body, which was yelling and crying apart?

She felt weak, with loose limbs under his grip.

His menacing features with glittering eyes made her strip

Of her virginity, between a cup and a lip.

She was bared, bruised and abused with filth.

She felt aggrieved, anguished and agonized.

Was this the truth of married life?

She was left blue, bleak, and crestfallen,

Despaired, disheartened, dispirited and discouraged.

She was compelled to a life of insignificance,

With endeavours planned but always hidden.

Living with herself in a house of misery,

Tormented by words of profanities.

Should she lie buried within the crevices of her black soul?

Or should she wake up with an optimistic, buoyant and sunny soul?

Her voice echoed, the tides will ebb away soon with each role.

To rise and bring the change she yearns to see as a whole.

She closed her eyes to wake each new morn,

Hiding her spirits behind her lovely smile.

Transformed from decay, desolation and despair,

She became a Survivor and not a victim in repair.

MOTHER

A mother gives birth to a child,

She cradles and cajoles,

She caresses and cures,

She nurtures and allures.

Mother is the epitome of love.

She is an angel pure as a dove.

She weathers all storms of life,

Facing obstacles with all her might.

She is the pillar of the house.

Standing firm, performing duties round the clock.

She is self-reliant and hopeful.

She is self-resisting and soulful.

She is an incarnation of beauty.

A nurse so devoted without any booty.

A Guardian angel who vigils with every click.

A guide who never desires to be rich.

A mother is a selfless worker.

She is an unpaid maid.

She bears the family brunt's but dredges.

Never complaining or bearing grudges.

A mother needs no Taj in her name.

She is bountiful and nameless.

An artist whose sketches are tameless.

A sculptor whose portraits are marvelous.

A mother can never be defined.

She is a figure who cannot be undermined.

People may leave you in a lurch,

But a mother will rescue you with her search.

She is the smallest Wren of your home.

But her presence is still measureless.

Pay homage to her with emotion.

She deserves your respect and devotion.

TRANQUILITY

Life is a sea of waves,

That ebbs and flows with the coming of tides.

Creating turbulence or tranquility,

Depending on the flow of time.

Our minds are divided into two hemispheres,

One locks and the other unlocks the key

To fathom the depths of hidden treasures,

Lying dormant in the cerebral hemispheres.

Our thoughts are like scrambled letters,

Untwining and unwinding crazy words.

Do we decipher their meaning in some concrete form?

Or do we play havoc with our lives.

Liberation? Where is liberation?

Is it in our minds or in the material world?

We lay waste our powers in opening closets,

Without unlocking the casket that buries the peaceful soul
alive.

We, humans face the upheavals of life,

Coated with stress and burdens of strife.

Never pausing to peep inside our souls,

To discover the golden jewel of peace within.

Peace, Ah! we meet you after traversing the course of life,

Nearing Death, which is a pause before life after death.

Still in dilemma of having attained full happiness in life,

But dying, with hopes of reaching eternity in peace.

MEMORIES

Memories are your ingrained food.

They are embedded in your soul's hood,

Because by birth your soul is burdened

With the memories of your past life.

Recollections of the past is the memoir of the present.

The smile on newborn face is the residue,

Of bygone years that remain obscure,

Without impacting the present life.

We lean on our stars and go by destiny.

Fated to govern the future of our lives.

Without creating a meaningful life,

That can live down the memory lane.

Life is like the coming of seasons,

Following the sequence that will follow reason.

Spring, Summer, Autumn, and Winter is

Like childhood, Adolescence, Maturity and Old age.

Memories create history.

As what happens in the present

Is scripture as past memoir,

To be recollected and remembered as repertoire.

You are no artist,

But yet you can paint the canvas of your life,

With hues of multifarious memories,

That imprints a happy or tragic picture of your life.

Memories are like bells that tinkle,

The sweet moments and happiness,

That amasses the wealth of your life.

And tune life's sweet notes of your lyre.

Memories can spill the clutter,

Of bad thoughts that weighs the burdened soul.

Making you feel uncanny and uneasy,

In traversing the unhappy moments of your life.

Memories are a treasure,

To be cajoled and caressed.

No matter, what magical transcriptions they contain,

The residue is forever a joy to retain.

Abide by your memories,

Let them linger and prolong,

For, the wisdom and experience they give

Helps you steer the voyage of your life's ship.

A STRANGER

Unaware of the line of your ancestry,

Unknown to the bundle of rituals,

Bewitched, caged in your own identity,

You are a stranger to yourself.

Breath breathes life into your living self.

Food and water nourish your body.

Clothes adorn and shelter you.

Culturally condoned, you are a stranger to yourself.

Devouring books sharpens your brain.

Communication aligns you with society.

Mastery in languages makes you voluble.

But alas! You are a stranger to yourself.

Parents are your guardian angels.

Teachers are your mentors in every angle.

Friends win your trust by being your confidante.

Oh! Who are you? A stranger to yourself.

Ignorance is bliss in your childhood.

Thoughtlessness is excused in your adolescence.

Prudence is exercised in your adulthood.

Crossing all bars in age, your soul still remains a stranger to yourself.

Mirror reflects your true self.

It is an identical twin of your personality.

Your laughter and smile disguise your internal hurts and despair.

Again, you become a stranger to yourself.

Awards and rewards give hopes to aspire.

Building a façade, living with lies to yourself.

Fame and power reduce you to ashes.

Burning with splinters, a stranger to yourself.

Passing school with flying colours infuses confidence.

Perseverance with toil in college builds solidarity.

Profession promotes the economy, giving you stability.

Still a Nobody, pleasing Everybody, a stranger to yourself.

Marriage binds two souls into an indissoluble knot.

Bearing children as fruits of your conjugal bond.

Building a home, nestling your siblings,

Behind this curtain of life, you remain a stranger to yourself.

Grow up! Have courage and look into yourself.

Peep through the doors of your inner self.

Download your true image from the mirror,

Feast on the Alma Mater, the Soul of yourself,

And No Long, remain a stranger to your Own Self!!

LONELINESS

Loneliness lodges itself in the psyche,

For it holds fast and never leaves.

Loneliness is most agonizing and anguishing,

Not in solitude but in companionship still languishing.

The paradox is of aging,

The elasticity is of time,

Which leads to the path of loneliness,

That becomes the key to our lasting relationship.

Loneliness infuses the agony of some terror,

Which fills the heart and mind with fear.

It is like seeing into the bottom of the vessel,

Creating a vacuum beyond some abstract.

Solitude fertilizes the imagination.

But loneliness empties it of vitality.

Loneliness sands the baseboards of the spirit,

With a scratchy restlessness of belongingness with merit.

Each one has a strange way of denying our loneliness.

Or confer validity upon the streaming existence.

It is a feeling that resides in the underworld or the sky,

Either denigrating or uplifting one so high.

Loneliness is a nuanced feeling in which,

The individual fights alone, all alone.

You are driven in the nescience of emptiness,

Till you are floating into acquiescence.

Loneliness is an interior chill,

Independent of externalities.

It is a warping of reality,

That is itself intensely, almost an unbearable variety.

You struggle and fight,

Between feelings of happiness and discomfort,

Between pervasive strains of rest and unrest,

Till you are aroused by eying the real self.

It is an acute sense of existence,

That binds an ultimate paean to the relationship,

Between loneliness and creative vitality,

Because it is the truth and the reality.

Cowards say loneliness leads to nothingness.

Hence, accepting a denial of their own self.

But artists seek a reality aroused by a spirit of creativity,

Driven away from loneliness and silence of this habitable world.

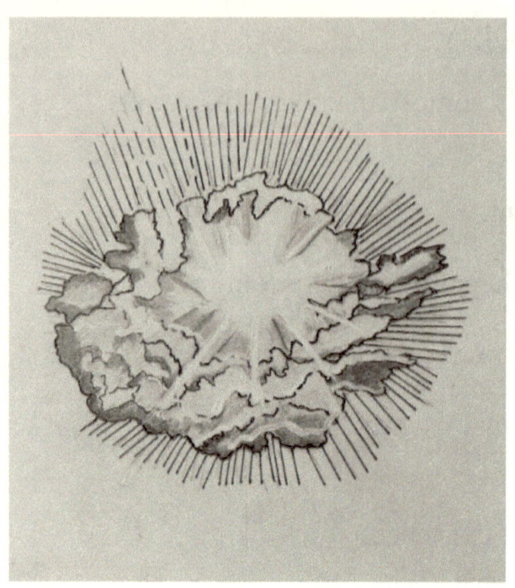

Clouds

Clouds are like tabula rasa,

Clear white blank sheets.

Where you can scribble your thoughts,

Turbulent and lying buried in the mind.

When they are gray in color,

They reflect your shades of moods.

Your gloominess, dullness and drowsiness

Warning to cover them with flowers of joy.

Black clouds raise a storm in our life,

Rustling, bustling and tormenting in strife.

Running hither, thither in stress and strain

Giving no tranquility of mind.

Ah! The bright orange morning clouds,

They infuse us with breath and sunshine.

Illuminating the triangles of life,

Nourishing the aura of the soul of mankind.

Clouds of red hue surmount the sky,

Sketching the horizon with blood and warmth.

Matching with red corpuscles spanning the veins,

Invigorating calmness, giving strength that reigns.

Patches of clouds that waver and quiver,

Like locks of wild hair let loose and high.

Winding and unwinding the streets of sky,

Raise a question of happiness in life.

O clouds! with your changing hues,

Spread out like a feathered blanket,

Entombing the whole world far and wide,

Forming an arch, shielding human life.

AMERICA

America is the U.S.A.

U are united we stand.

S is a state of sacred hearts.

A is the Divine Altar.

The roads are winding pathways,

That traverses in zigzag ways.

It is really like you sweep from a pedestal,

And fall with a swing, sloping from a hill.

The swishing sounds of the cars,

Slash by every second.

Holding your breath is a legend,

But they flash by with a blink in a second.

The "Legacy" is a world of Bollywood,

People walking like celebrities.

Mimicking and dancing and rollicking,

Like stars who need monitoring.

The houses stand in a line,

Resembling a line of hedgerows.

Facing each other with a smile,

With two green trees as stalwarts on either side.

The grass is like a green carpet,

Laid out in front of each house.

The gardens and parks are spread out,

With green grasslands and beds of flowers.

Water parks, aquariums, and gymnasiums,

Abounds in each community.

Tracing the movements of bikers with helmets,

As if, moving out for mountaineering.

ATMs stand out on the road,

Without the menace of guards and watchmen.

Gas stations give a blank and bleak look,

Sans the queue of customers in a brook.

The traffic rules are strictly adhered,

Without a breach of any custom ever heard.

The morning trespassers follow the side lane,

Greeting every stranger with warmth on the pedestrian.

America is the nation of economic growth and power,

That surpasses the wealth of others and empowers.

Stand as a stalwart to the nation,

But never forget the roots of your destination.

DREAMS

Dreams are a visage,

That trace the features of our age,

Outlining our desires on the canvas,

Of our life which we paint with grace.

Dreams emanates from our conscious mind,

Surfacing our hopes that combat behind,

Prompting us to have faith,

Because wishes are like horses to win the race.

Night envelopes darkness,

Making the world go asleep in harness.

The subconscious mind dances to tunes,

That plays with music of hope raising sand dunes.

Morning dawns with new aspirations,

Ready to combat with all tribulations.

Our efforts seem to go in vain,

When negativity floods our mind without gain.

We cry in pain, but dream in vain.

Soothing our minds with sagacious sanity,

Following them with a veracity,

Trying to capture it in a day with ferocity.

Dreams are a necessity.

They give you mental fulfillment.

But translating them in reality,

Makes you live with tranquility.

Never forsake your dream.

Love them, live them,

Fulfill them, laying close to your heart,

For they transpose your spirits with great art.

ETERNAL BONDAGE

Marriage is the bond of two hearts, and two souls.

It is a sacred temple which holds the idols,

Of opposite genders migrating from different sources,

Traversing two paths which merge in one course.

Nalini and Prabhat are two tributaries of the same river,

That meander through diverse rocks,

Reaching uphill and downhill in their paths of life,

Without the consciousness of flowing together and reaching
the same banks.

Medical Science teaches you, your bodily existence.

Airlines teach you to soar high, reaching zeniths.

Science and Technology join hands to make amendments,

In life's journey filled with joys and tribulations.

On January 22nd a vow was pledged between Nalini and
Prabhat,

Piercing the two hearts with red roses of love.

Making promises of holding hands of

Faith and trust leading to eternal bondage.

The red corpuscles oozed out with crimson blood of passion,

Dying the black soot of planes, weaving a flowery bed,

Full of fragrance of love, compassion and new hopes,

Singing the melodies of togetherness in lyrical ropes.

The seeds of love blossomed into two flowers.

Bonding into two songs of love, Geetika and Geetanjali.

Goldie and Guriya radiating wealth of new fortune,

Breathing life and emanating eminence with new tones.

Both soared their wings high into the heavens,

Fulfilling promises and gaining prominence.

Leading a diasporic life, being settled abroad.

Giving birth to flowers that shine like copious stars, for sure.

The untiring efforts of a doctor and a housewife,

Tried to make life a bed of roses.

The humility and strength of an engineer held the
strongholds,

Never wavering, but holding the pillars of household with
fortitude.

The human bonding is like a spring garden,

Where love and hope blossoms like beautiful flowers,

Even when some aspirations age and wither unheeded,

Million others sprout and keep the bond forever.

GURU AND SHISHYA BONDAGE

Guru and Shishya are two terms,

Interlocked in communion with each other.

They exist without any barriers,

For it knows no bondages and boundaries.

Guru and Shishya is a Presence,

That graces us with freedom, belongingness,

Stillness, fullness, passion and love.

Instilling a bondage which is fearless in essence.

Life on this earth abounds with do's and don'ts,

This decorum exists only in the eyes of the external world.

A true relationship between the Guru and Shishya

Abounds in love with no judgements.

The pilgrimage of shishya's life is Dhyan,

Which culminates and begins at the feet of his Guru.

Every word uttered by Guru is a Mantra,

A codified energy that leads to Moksha.

Moksha means a renunciation of this materialistic world.

Devoutness and devotion to the Guru is the renunciation of
the self.

Liberation of the soul is just an illusion,

For Guru is the ultimate wisdom of Divine creation.

Guru awakens awareness to the Vasanas,

Our latent tendencies lie dormant within us.

Dissolution of evils happens through deep surrender,

By the grace of Guru's compassion and love.

Guru is Brahma, without four heads,

Guru is Vishnu, without four arms,

Guru is Shiva, without three eyes.

Guru is Par-A-Brahma, which remains unmanifest.

The divinity in the relationship designs,

The herbs that grow is Sanjeevani booti,

The air we breathe is the Pranavayu,

The food served is Prasad of the Divine,

The water consumed is Amrit.

A Guru abstains from materialism.

He opens the doorways of subtler dimensions.

He exudes the glow and attraction of Yog,

His words become magical and Divine manifestations.

Do we find devoted shishya in contemporary times?

Who possesses this divine wisdom of Guru Tattva?

Can they absolve their ills and evils,

Effortlessly through the intention and attention of their
Divine Guru?.

We are caught in the web,

Of our own distortions and Karmic patterns.

Our we able to amplify our happiness,

Fearlessly, without effort from our sense organs?

Meditation and Yoga with your Guru,

Manifests abundance and fullness within and without.

Which assimilates knowledge, translating into wisdom,

Awakening your soul, releasing energies and rejuvenating
your true Self.

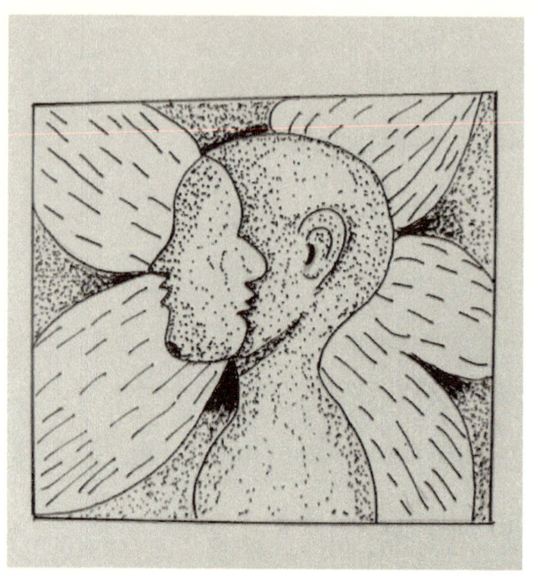

INTROSPECTION

Who am I?

Is the multimillionaire question?

That torments our soul?

Leading to introspect our true self.

Woe besides! Peep inside!

Our thoughts lie embedded,

Like the moss on the grass.

Bright and glossy but sticky inside.

Introspection is self-reflection.

Of our sensory, bodily, cognitive and emotional states.

Our five senses give us perception and recognition,

But our brain is a testimonial of our observations.

We determine our goals in life.

Pursuance of it leads to passion.

Passion deters us to fall in line with reason,

But our conscience aligns with any treason.

Our present thoughts play

Hide and seek with the past.

Painting our emotions in black and white,

Making us aware of the truth with the naked eye.

We wear a smile to please others,

Being a nervous hypocrite by lying to oneself.

We put up a façade of goodness and goodwill,

Denying transparency of true spirit with ill will.

Our dreams spell our true worth.

Our facts deny the reality.

Our stress is our instability,

And our distress is our unreliability.

Let us use our inner eyes as spectacles,

With a larger frame and crystal-clear glasses,

To solve and resolve all precarious issues,

That breaks the life pattern's tissues.

Reach out and traverse through,

The maze of our embedded thoughts.

Scrutinize, analyze, criticize our own self,

To reveal a replica of our true self.

Introspect and see the Divine within,

For God resides in the walls of our heart.

Pray to the Holy Spirit to keep you sublime,

For introspection of self-leave stalwarts behind.

LAZINESS

How do you define laziness?

I define as " On Doing Nothing"

Lying flat on your back,

Looking up with a blank,

Caressing your mind with nothingness.

A child plays pranks, avoids work,

Shirks studies, gets spanked,

For being a pain in the neck.

Running hither, thither, just for heck

For ravaging the sacrimony of keeping abreast.

Being lousy, lumpy, crazy artifact,

Earns the honor of wasting craft,

On trivial things, meaningless to others,

But, complimenting himself with accolades from mother,

As lazy as the pig, but a darling boy for brother.

Laziness and Idleness are synonyms,

Complimenting each other as a phenomenon,

Working together, aspiring with zest,

To outdo each other, without a mess,

Bowing in humbleness to be the best.

The world is up and doing

Crackling its nerves, outreaching for something,

Forever in disagreement, never at peace,

Raging with discords, waging a roar,

Creeping of laziness can endstop a war.

Our minds are like Devils,

Overactive, manipulative and scheming.

Overburdened with stress, leading to distress.

Happy are those who keep in their nest,

Being calm and caressed, by being at rest,

Releasing their tensions, to be at their best.

The world is a rat race.

Scurrying to dig holes at their pace.

Cement the walls of your house,

Dare not pull strings of others lounge,

Energize your strength, relax your nerves,

Never cross latitude, but capture your curbs.

Exercise economy, in effort

Stop an overdraft from your bank of work,

Be repulsive of taking a loan from your resource,

Always count on the income of your source,

By utilizing 'Lazy' as a fixed cause.

Laziness can cause anxiety.

Shakes you with fever,

Makes you tremble and shiver.

Because the people raise their eyes,

With a question to your identity in life.

But the heart stays cool, unperturbed with hostility.

Your wealth is your wisdom,

To fulfill the needs of your kingdom.

Never falter to take precocious steps,

That trespasses the inactivity of your life.

For you are sure in failure of your strife,

Voila! be content as lazy as a ship in the doldrums.

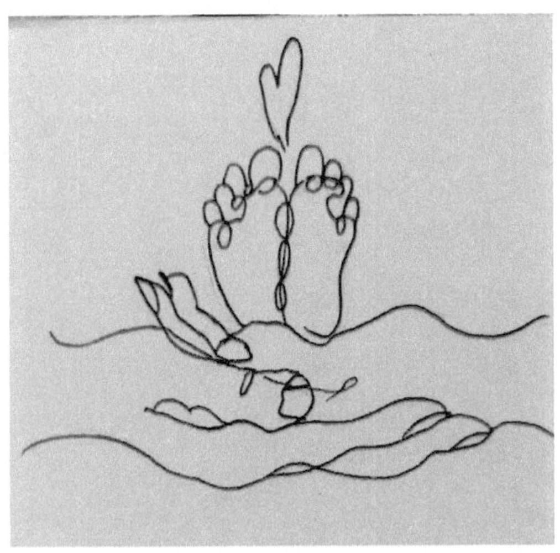

LOVE

Love is like a sweet candy.

When chewed, it tastes sweet?

When love turns sour, it becomes bitter.

Making you passionate and embittered.

Love is like sweet honey.

It becomes more precious than money.

Love arouses high hopes,

Which knot into rough ropes.

Love has no depth.

It is fathomless, sturdy and stealth.

Love has no weight.

It's healthy and light and harbours no hate.

Love has power.

It can change sides every hour.

Love abounds in wealth.

Which cherishes and sustains your health.

Love has no dimensions.

All calculators fail to mention.

Love is measureless.

No scale can match its happiness.

Love is ageless.

It grows in passion, experience and wisdom.

Love is endless.

It is beyond death, boundless.

Love pines for more and more.

The fever and the fret make you sore.

Love eradicates evil.

And rescues you from every peril.

Days march towards night.

Sunrise is followed by sunset.

Like the river and soft blowing breezes,

Love flows freely and never ceases.

Love is Sweet.

Love is Glorious.

Love is Divine.

Never forsake it, hold it and make it Eternal.

OH! SKYSCRAPERS

Skyscrapers are an iconic part of the skyline,

They are the model of the timeline.

They stand like pillars, tall and straight

Like intensive posters of the land.

Each floor of Skyscraper is a storey in a box,

With squares and triangles of rooms jutting out.

Equipped with sliding doors which move across,

Fleeting up and down like a sea -shore.

Each storey surmounts on top of the other,

Like close cropped rungs of the ladder.

Houses are not homes but each is a "Flat"

With rooftops that do not match with a mat.

Flats are like identical twins,

Looking alike in space, maze and every link.

Standing in a row like hedges in straight line,

Strengthened with molten bricks, steel and lime.

Elevators float you from first to last floor,

Sailing smoothly like a swift wind.

Each building holds a community of its own,

Forming a Township, harboring great souls.

Skyscrapers master big Companies and gigantic Malls,

That buzz with activities round the clock.

Multitudes swarm in like busy bees,

Trying to draw the honey of life from wealthy seas.

Skyscrapers shine with glowing lights in the night,

Illuminating the towers without any fright.

Life becomes mechanical, moving like robots,

Becoming expressionless, as if in sabotage.,

Skyscrapers give fresh air and ventilation,

But they tend to isolate people with their omnipresence.

They are ornate and embellished from outside,

But passionless and hollow from every side.

Each skyscraper has its own story.

Like fairies and devils of Arabian Nights.

Beauty is like a beast with multifarious flaws,

Unveiling the truth without any laws.

Oh! Skyscrapers, do not curtail the bounty of life,

Sprouting hither and thither like unwanted weeds
everywhere.

Your enormity and breadth tarnish the beauty of life,

Stopping nature to spread its wings far and wide.

OUR EARTH

Earth is the soul of life.

Earth has power to hold us tight,

Earth is the flamboyant art,

That displays the universe with her heart.

Geographically, the earth is round.

Historically, the earth is bound,

With wealth of facts and fiction

That heralds the world with its diction.

Earth is our mother.

It cradles its species in its womb.

Bearing and transgressing all afflictions.

Striving to survive with each benediction.

Beauty abounds in Nature.

Where mountains, meadows, forests and hillsides,

Slope and slant with transformations on each side.

Planting seeds in beds for growth far and wide.

Earth gives you manna.

She drenches you with a shower.

Nobody can question her will power,

That can play havoc or bless you each hour.

The Earth is round.

With an immeasurable circumference.

Each quarter and a half a radius,

Floats with life's music melodiously.

The Sun is her travelling lamp.

The Moon is her beacon of fluorescent light.

The clouds are her ray of hope.

The stars are her silver lining to each goal.

The rivers flow meticulously.

The forests stretch with density.

The blue sky entombs the earth

Providing a rooftop over the berth.

The flowers emanate their sweet fragrance.

Their diverse colours paint the canvas of the earth.

Giving a picturesque beauty of birth,

Breathing life in living organisms full of worth.

The droning of bees flitting on flowers.

The humming of crickets in odd hours.

The chirping of birds in each dower,

Create an orchestral symphony on Earth's bower.

We owe allegiance to our Mother Earth,

By wishing her prosperity and benevolence,

Blessing her to remain Evergreen and Everlasting,

Because she cradles all humanity till eternity.

PATRIOTIC INDEPENDENCE

Being patriotic is honing virtues,

Of loyalty, courage, honesty with many more hues,

In being a veteran to show faithfulness to your nation,

Without understanding the depth of the notion.

Soldiers have laid down their lives to give freedom,

To their beloved country and many stand with dignity,

Bowing in humility for those who sacrificed their lives,

Across the borders to stop access to the invaders.

Today we hold our heads in pride,

Reminiscing the honours earned in ride,

To flaunt the glory of the nation won galore,

Without the guilt of rummaging the dark clouds abhorred.

To me, being patriotic is helping the poor, sore,

Handicapped, deprived of livelihood, standing in awe.

A beam of light shines through his life,

As he catches the glimpse of hope and support from the
patriotic strife.

A blind man needs to cross the road,

A beggar begs alms without having arms,

Old parents are ditched on streets by prodigal son,

A dying soul yearns for water for her last breath.

A divine soul turns patriotic when he joins hands,

To offer help and satiate the dire needs of others.

Showers himself with blessing by nurturing poor,

Manifesting a ray of hope in every soul, brother.

Patriotic was Ashoka the great,

Who renounced bloodshed and war.

To bring renunciation and reconciliation in life,

Teaching Buddhism and divinity amongst mankind.

Patriotic policemen like Arun Jadhav, in 26/11 Taj Hotel attack.

Tough, non-fussy, daring, who came out alive in the carnage,

Where he chased militants, gangsters and extortionists.

With his unfathomable belief "The God looks after us."

Independence is not flying Triranga,

Independence is not saluting the martyrs,

Independence is not mourning the dead past,

Independence is igniting the fire of freedom for humanity.

India is now a superpower, where stood a unity tower.

Definitions of patriotism may differ,

But the idea will always be the same,

Be Human, Caring and instill Love to restore faith with sanity.

RELATIONSHIPS

We all board on the ship of life,

With a free will to ride in a tide,

Weathering the storms with tranquil calm,

With the support of relations holding their palms.

Each one by birth is related to mother,

Father, brother, sister, cousins and others.

Without knowing the potential of meaning

Of values, virtues, nature of relations assuming.

The food for relationship is love,

To nurture it we need appreciation,

To strengthen it, demands resolution,

Bonding together needs communication.

Love is a fallacy, it ties and unties,

The mutual bonds with a lie,

With pretense of unfathomable passion,

Making you live in an illusion.

Nature is the best teacher,

That teaches the bonds of relationship.

A Long queue of ants walk in a row,

Supporting and catering the needs of each without woe.

An owl to an owlet, a duck to a duckling,

A calf to a cow, a kitten to a cat,

Establishes the unblemished relations,

Between a mother and a sibling.

With time the young ones take wings to fly,

Leaving their nests, soaring new heights,

Their silence in relationships

Speaks volumes designating connection.

Laughter, smiles, cries and tears,

Are expressions of emotions which bear,

The brunt of knots tied in human relationship,

And end in perennial discords in associations.

Deliverance of passions ends in turmoil.

Establishing the myth of trustworthy relation,

For a smiling face smothers a fire

In the heart, whose flames in mankind go haywire?

We become myopic in our vision,

Instead of assessing our strengths and weaknesses,

Ignoring moral issues when implications are toddler size,

We reap perilous giant-size repercussions.

Broken homes, failures in marriage,lead to

Seclusion,alienation, isolation and separation.

They are reminders to prune our negative traits,

Establishing a positive mind-set with affirmation.

Overcoming peccadilloes with grace,

Administering corrections from God with a straight face.

For God is at work in life's interrelation,

Prioritizing self control as the master key of all relations.

BELOVED

My dear beloved, I wish you in the fabric of your life,

Colors of true happiness, love and enterprise,

Loads of amazing surprises, moments of joy and merriment,

Enlightening your days with new hopes and contentment.

May your life be filled with effulgence,

Your nights give you peace and incandescence.

And the golden rays of sun spread their phosphorescence,

Sparkling your virtues with radiance.

Your mind reverberates with the music of life,

That vibrates the lyrics of your work for mankind.

Your daily moods vacillate with hope and sheen,

Illuminating your life with splendour and gleam.

You are a sweetheart, who is so loving and kind,

A blessed soul like you, I could not find.

I cherish the goodness ingrained in you,

That makes you my mentor and beacon of light.

Your addiction to mobile is simply perplexing,

Which defeats my love, suffocating and suffixing,

The messages that keep flitting through each moment,

Keeping you more occupied than your spouse's endearments.

Your presence throughout the day,

Gives strength to all that comes your way

May you reach your goal in all you strive,

Overcoming all the pitfalls of your life.

You are persevering in every endeavour,

Making things match with great favour,

Your eyes are focused on your goal,

That never leads you astray from your soul.

Your garden of life may bloom with roses,

Leading you to a right path by the grace of Moses.

Your caressing touch is like a benediction,

That cures mankind of all its affliction.

God help those who help themselves.

Is an adage you teach oneself.

Abiding conscientiously with the principles of life,

Putting yourself first in securing your position with might.

MIRROR

Mirror is never an Error,

It is the true reflection without any measure.

But mirror can be a terror,

Because it scales the truth with fervour.

Mirror looks as clear as crystal,

Made of glass of different lustre,

All geometrical figures of mirror give shades,

To every object reflected in a maze.

Mirror is the variety of life.

Man can turn an angel or adopt a vice.

Winning the world with all lies mingle,

And laying bare his powers in shingles.

Beauty is truth, truth is beauty.

Is an appropriate maxim for the mirror,

This material world may forsake you,

But you seek shelter in the mirror review.

Mirror is an incredible invention,

Opening the doors of each detection.

Your picture becomes an inverted image,

When your upended self surpasses your lineage.

Fairy tales depict the charm of magical mirrors,

Wavering the wicked queen's mind with vengeance,

But Snow- White replies with consolation,

Kindness pays but vanity gives exultation.

Mirror reflects a history of life.

Ancient monuments and transcriptions,

Are a mirror of old ages,

Beholding our past with tales from sages.

Religion teaches us to introspect,

Materialism promises to prosper with all assets,

Spiritualism instructs to search your soul,

Because the soul is the mirror that reflects your goal.

Mirror gives transparency to your innate self.

Sanning, analyzing and comprehending your own elf.

Know then thyself and not learn to scan,

For Mirror is the true reflection of man.

WINDOWS

My name is "Windows",

I am built in every habitation,

"Wind" my first part is vital,

With "ows", I complete every recital.

I am the ventilator of the house,

Peeping in every nook and corner.

The wind swishes past me,

Giving breath to people, with no expectation to see.

I am present in variegated colours,

Brown, peach, maroon and black,

You will find me in every size,

Round, square, rectangle, oval in every hack.

I am perched with a variety of vases,

Blooming with multi-coloured flowers,

Effusing a sweet fragrance that adorns,

Each breath with a boom.

I am laced with creepers,

Glossy green, surmounting in length and breadth.

Money plants, with their heart-shaped leaves,

Traces the wealth of people who stealthily weave.

My freedom is curbed,

With glass window panes,

Which are transparent or translucent,

Hindering the breeze to enter each vent.

I brave the brunt of nature.

Tempests and storms never spare my stature.

My hinges squeak, my glass panes clutter,

My heart aches and cries with a splutter.

Each domicile or an abode,

Has a window as an edifice.

A habitat with my absence,

Is like a mind without sense.

I am, the window of the human mind,

That sneaks and peeks from behind.

Denial of my presence by human reason,

Will make a man commit many treasons.

I am the window to God.

Prayers, offerings and benediction,

All fail to keep their promissory note,

Unless the sacred window to my soul promotes.

I, at last peep through the clouds into the heaven,

Searching the abode of Almighty in every condominium,

Because God you carved and moulded me,

To give breath and meaning to every minion.

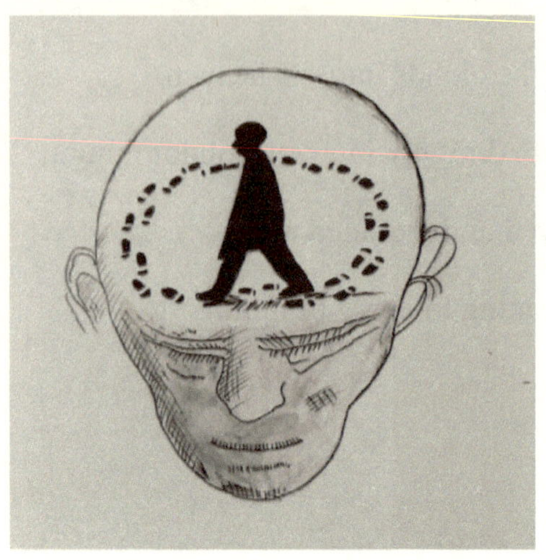

THOUGHTS

Thoughts are like raindrops,

They pitter, patter, up and down,

Like pebbles dashing on the shore,

Leaving footprints on sand galore.

Thoughts are unorganized,

Needing to be framed with purpose,

Like bead sown in a necklace,

Looking focused and center-faced.

Thoughts and emotions are interconnected,

They are tied together with a strong bond.

Happiness exhilarates you mentally,

Sorrow disturbs you sadistically.

When learning is purposeful, creativity blossoms,

When creativity blooms, thinking emanates.

When thinking triggers, knowledge is enlightened,

When knowledge is lit, satisfaction is brightened.

Dreams are transposed into thoughts,

Thoughts in turn result in action.

Action leads to self-discipline,

Which transforms life with gratification.

When thoughts go astray,

They wander through the caves of the dungeon.

Hark! a magic wand needs to be finite,

To kindle the spark of light infinite.

Treacherous thoughts are emitted by feeble mind,

Making the soul commit untold crimes.

Punishment becomes the timely recourse,

To subdue the soul with sweet discourse.

Innocent thoughts of a child are vulnerable,

They are spontaneous, innate and unblemished.

They speak the truth without hesitation,

Because it is spoken without temptation.

Thoughts of an adolescence play hide and seek,

With parents, siblings, friends and neighbors meek.

Reason is tossed towards heaven,

Mocking the world, having no haven.

Thoughts get refined with maturity,

Tempered with reason and authority.

Counseling and advices taper the mind,

Giving you strength to look behind.

Thoughts with age is spiced with experience,

Giving you wisdom to practice before you preach.

Shouldering your burden with a might,

Bowing with grace, spreading a smile.

RE-AWAKENING

Oh! Where are my wings?

Cried the Owlet out of the ring,

You will soon grow to fly and swing,

But Mama, Time makes my wings wring.

The pain of waiting is becoming endemic,

With the panic of Corona Pandemic,

Its outbreak is more than Epidemic,

For the havoc caused in the world is distressing.

Farmers have to labour hard to till the soil,

Students have to find success with toil,

Businessmen without profit seem to recoil,

Children have to bear this stupendous turmoil.

Each new patient is living in dread,

Doctors are exercising their rights with might,

Watchmen are keeping vigilant without fight,

Leaders are ready to face the project with foresight.

The Lockdown gives us a mild solution,

But it gives our lives no resolution,

Locking ourselves physically with earnestness,

Mentally helps to face Carona with staunchness.

"Mama" cried the Owlet, it is awful,

Yes, facing the trauma is fearful,

The cost of precious lives in this war is dreadful,

Hoping for the conquest of disease is direful.

Each individual is living in disguise,

Children and elders are having time to beguile,

Creativity is budding in all walks of life,

To utilize time and make them mentally preoccupied.

A time was when Adam and Eve also enjoyed the fruits of evil,

Oh! Humans were you not then so civil,

The scourge of Corona is not there to make you lame,

But your freedom at home has made you maimed.

Cry! Cry! My beloved country for cure,

The Almighty will definitely come to succour,

My dear Owlet, time is not far when Corona will bury in disgrace,

The world will be re-awakened to live peacefully in grace.

THE TRIALS OF LIFE

Life is not a bed of roses,

I am not born with a silver spoon to pose.

It's only when I close my eyes,

I see the future as clear and bright.

But with the passage of time,

I falter my path and go astray,

The ladder I chose to climb,

Makes me fall down with time.

The Jackals of life painted that ladder of success,

With dark demeaning colours,

Achieving glory meant satisfying lust,

Of greedy Boars who betray my trust.

I am simple,

I am honest,

I am studious,

I am persevering,

But do these qualities define life?

They only trigger you towards a dark pitch,

In contemporary times which devour you,

Fool you and target your soul.

Whispering promises of making Heaven on Earth.

I blink away the tears of remorse,

When struck with time's force of penitence.

The ray of hope starts receding,

When I fall victim to evil, succeeding.

I succumbed, I yielded, I fell.

But the demons did not lift me.

The inner voice gave a screeching yell,

And uplifted me to cast a spell.

I rose, I stood, I saw,

The Divine spirit at my door.

Be brave, be bold, be strong,

To stand the Trials of life.

LOST BIRD

I lost my parents when I was five,

And I felt like a bird, caged for life,

At the hands of my uncle and his wife,

Being fed and slaughtered with the edge of a knife.

The innocent eyes used to peep in fear,

The dread and violence mingled,

With the unknown that lay very near,

At the anguished destiny of an aggrieved bird.

Promises are made to be fulfilled,

I was trapped in the nest with barbed wires,

Caught in the hands of menacing liars,

Who made me dance to the tune of their desires.

The fearful night when I lay in the lap,

Of clenched hands, a smouldering tongues of fire,

Burned my bones and freckled my skin with scars,

Within the clutches of volcanic desire.

It tore my soul, laid me bare, without breath,

The hand that touched me was hard and rough,

That inflicted blisters, bloody red and tough,

I was hypnotized, captivated and plagiarized,

Lying listless and helplessly in brutal hands.

I died every day of my life,

Unknown to the pleasures of childhood,

The death of the so-called caretakers,

Made me a puppet in the hands of traitors.

I became a freelancer,

Moving from tree to tree like a lost bird,

Failed to grow up emotionally, physically and mentally,

For the sexual abuse left those,

Indelible scars on my life,

That could not be eradicated easily.

They were deep sore wounds,

Bleeding, shedding, molten of fire,

Like a volcano ready to erupt,

With the flood of tears, sealed with voices corrupt.

The two arms those were next to me,

Encircled and cajoled and caressed,

Soon became the claws of the monster,

Made me tremble with my own voice,

Strangling, suffocating, smothering my laughter.

Will the lost bird find justice?

To heal the blemishes upon her soul.

Or will she rap on the doors of heaven?

To question the Almighty Power for compensation?

LITTLE ANGEL

God gifted me with a little Angel.

Her name was Shanaya,

She had pink cheeks,

Rosy lips, pointed chin,

With curly hair atop her head.

She wriggled and curled,

Twisted and turned,

Snuggled in mother's bosom,

Sucking the milk with glory,

Breathing the warmth with jest.

Her long leg sprawled in the lap,

Her soft hands made a fist,

Her fingers twirled under the mittens,

Her hair formed a mat over her head,

And her eyes peeped meekly, with nothing said.

She fluttered her wings in the early dawn,

Cried and yawned in the afternoon sunlight,

Breathed her presence in the evening twilight,

And twinkled like a star in bright moonlight.

Making us all proud by coming into the limelight.

We welcomed our princess with open arms,

Cuddled and caressed with loving charm,

Her very presence relinquished all the pain the mother bore,

For she was a blessed Angel who filled with delight,

In the life of parents and sister with all might.

SOLITUDE

Solitude is your soul self,

It walks with you,

Talks with you,

Smiles with you,

Plays with you,

And laughs with you.

Oh! my dear soul come close to me,

Capture and encase me peremptorily.

Let not it escape temporally,

But be engaged within my heart permanently.

Ah! Thou soul of thy sole self,

Meandering through the sea of life,

Recognize my true self in strife,

With the passions of mind all alive.

My partner is with me in distance,

My children are occupied with eminence,

My grandchildren are busy with their education,

My parents in my dream remain a manifestation

Knowledge is a process of give and take.

The more you impart, the more you receive.

It is a treasure that never recedes,

Rather it fills the foison of your mind and grows.

But solitude takes you miles away,

Deep in the heart it creates recesses,

It is like a solitary kite flying in the air,

Without knowing its destination.

Solitude teaches you to love yourself,

It ignites the spark of your inner spirit.

It sparkles and shines with the magic wand of seclusion,

That breathes in you the beauty of alienation.

You feel devoid of togetherness,

Happy in your forlornness,

No heartaches with remoteness,

But contented silence in your wilderness.

I seek the pleasure of solitude,

It encompasses my heart with fortitude.

The warmth of my blood never desires in longitude,

To reach out for companions with attitude.

Bereavement, loss, love and weariness,

Are strangers to my heart,

For I gather up in arms my own true self,

And peep within its tresses for peace and quietude.

Solitude, you are my sole treasure,

Free from fears and traumas of access,

To fame, glory and wealth of ingress,

Therefore, Arise, Awake and hold steadfast your sole self!!!

BELONGING

The very word is hyphenated, Be -Longing.

'Be' is the positive presence,

'Longing', circling the desire,

Joining hands together,

It displays possessiveness.

'Self' is undermined,

Where lies the word 'Mine'?

Mingling of virtues in life makes you virtuous,

But does virtuosity give you be-longing?

Your home is not your home.

Your parents are half way with you.

You are bridled to the house of another,

Which you nurture as your 'Own'.

Still, you do not belong.

Your decisions are not strong.

You are not a party in the throng.

Never exercise your mind too long.

Self-decision makes you overbearing.

Standing alone reproofs your Independence.

Working with men establishes your audacity.

Giving in, makes you succumb to humility.

You are a doll in your father's house.

A sheer partner with your spouse.

Mother of your children is a Provider,

A caretaker, a mentor,

Who sacrifices her 'Self' and never retires to nurture.

Your son gets married and brings a wife.

Your daughter finds a partner to bear the strife.

Your grandsons belong to you to shower love,

Your granddaughters identify with you like small doves.

You raise your eyes to question "Yourself",

Who are you? Where do you belong?

The tender heart that is mine,

Whispers quietly "No where".

The day's journey will be over.

The night curfew bell will ring.

Walking in the footpath of sands,

I will reach my end,

Without ever "Be-Longing"!!

Dread of Corona

Do I strike lightning?

With the coming of frightening

Corona, that creeps slowly and lightly,

And catches hold of your body tightly.

You shiver with fever,

Gives you the symptoms of mild cough and cold.

Your head aches and your mind swirls,

With the performance of the rapid Antigen test.

Internally you are hale and hearty,

But your anti-inflammatory viral,

Turn your Antigen test to positive,

Declaring you to be an infected Corona patient.

You have to remain within doors hush-hush.

You refrain from looking at others with shush-shush.

Hide your face under the mask,

Talking with others momentarily is a task.

You are looked down with derogation,

Symptomatic with high infection.

You are contaminated with a contagious disease,

Prone to spread its snares everywhere with ease.

The neighbourhood looks in awe at you.

They avert their eyes if you smile at them.

Cordial greetings is an avowed ban,

Your very presence is a fearful dread.

Your child is not contaminated,

But she has to face the brunt.

She has to refrain from playing with friends.

Participation in normal activity is a curse in the end.

Isolation is your only security,

Ah! Do not peep out of your room,

Your imposed restrictions will not allow,

To make you trespass others' ground.

You are under quarantine of fourteen days,

Like a phantom caged under the norms of Corona.

You become the butt of every gaze,

In the asylum of your own walls.

Silence is the keyword.

Live in quietude, seek no herd,

Sleep in peace, refrain from perturbation,

Self indulgence overcomes your consternation.

People look askance at you.

You are ridden with guilt.

But your innocence speaks volumes,

Am I a sinner you dread?

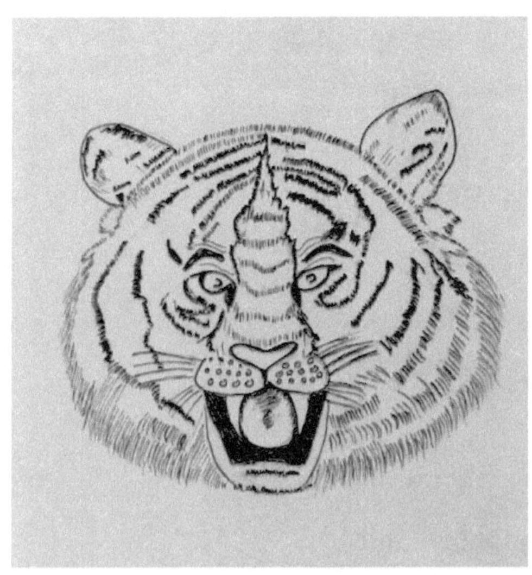

FEAR

Where the mind is without fear?

Can you hear it with your ear?

The journey of life traverses,

With upheavals here and there.

Life is shrouded in a bundle of mysteries.

A mother welcomes the birth of her child,

But fears the baby steps taken by might,

Being possessive and apprehensive with fright.

Life is fraught with tribulations.

Will we overcome them with adulations?

Will the parts of the body function in merriment?

And not decay in life's detriment?

Going to school is a pleasure.

Appearing for exams is a terror.

Climbing each rung of the ladder,

Is it fraught with errors?

Having courage to take a venture,

Makes you run through the venture,

Erupting goose pimples, qualms and jitters,

Will I accomplish it, filling me with fritters?

Degrees, Gold medals, Trophies lead to disquietude.

Because they apprehend the threat of solitude.

Achieving them forebodes incertitude,

Striving to possess those needs effort with quietude.

Marriages are made in heaven,

But they are earthly bonds with vows seven.

They steer the ship of life without consternation,

But the vicissitudes in life are never without perturbation.

Love, faith, compassion and courageousness,

Culminates the conjugal life with dauntlessness.

Children bridge this gap with boldness,

By their fearlessness, gallantry, impudence and doughtiness.

Wealth, Health, Prosperity and happiness,

Are they all the companions of the soul?

Is the soul, a spirit in search of hope?

Seeking Peace, Eternal Peace without scope.

Basking in toll free life with daily bread,

Torments the memory, the warder of the brain with dread.

Apprehensions, conflicts and tensions are the tools,

That turns the milk sour for fools.

The journey of life will get over, why fear death?

It shall steal your heart and leave you bereft.

The soul, lying buried will leave your life in a moment,

Unscathed, unheard, upward to Hell or Heaven.

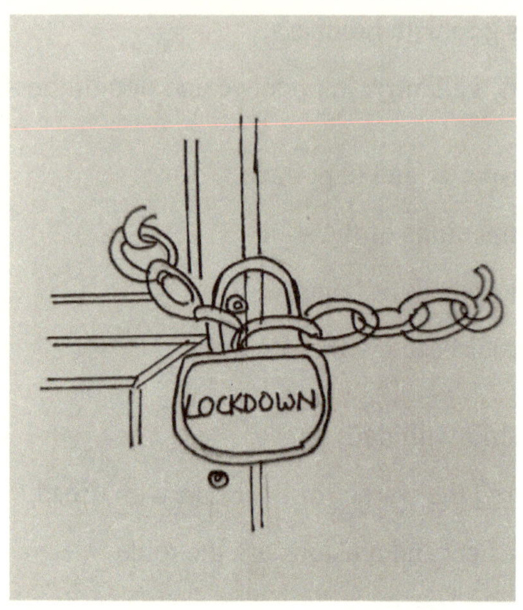

LOCKDOWN

Twenty-Twenty begins a New Year.

Springs a new life with no fear.

Joy, Hope, Happiness, Faith has no dearth

Because life seems so full of mirth.

January passes, February begins and March slowly creeps in,

Woe betides! What lies beneath?

Corona comes with a bang!

Gliding stealthily in each corner with slang.

Corona? Who is this Corona?

It is a large family of viruses,

Causing illness from common cold to Conjunctivitis,

It hijacks healthy cells and takes command,

Eventually, latches its spiky surface running rampant.

Government declares a Lockdown,

Casting a spell on mankind.

Relationships are neatly intertwined,

Mixed with moans, groans and whines.

Mind has become a blank sheet.

Dread, fear, anxiety are only there to take heed.

Corona has taken wings,

Spreading its snares globally like caved rings.

Beware of your neighbourhood,

Refrain from holding hands,

Curtail yourself in showing postures

Of love, affection or close gestures.

Outside food is prohibited.

Life at home is restricted.

Expression of love is truly inhibited.

Making your arteries constricted.

Home' is the real seclusion.

Abide within, stay indoors and be in reclusion.

Work from Home, be On-line,

Do not panic but together dine.

"What is this life so full of care?

We have no time to stand and stare."

Carona is here to refute the above adage,

For this pandemic gives ample time to adhere.

"Distances make the heart grow fonder"

Announcement of social distancing is an order.

To connect virtually and be mentally broader,

Learn to live and gracefully grow older.

Twenty-One surpasses over Twenty-Twenty,

Breathing a sigh of relief eventually,

But beware! Corona spreads like a wildfire,

Snatching lives in devastating attire.

Isolation, Desolation and Alienation in the wilderness of
Corona,

Make 'Quarantine' within your own home.

Confine yourself around its four walls,

Don't crib for celebrations in palatial halls.

Media, Newspaper and T.V. are all yelling,

'Be safe,' 'take care', and 'don't move', without spelling,

The medical recourse for Carona affliction,

Who is out of breath without oxygenation?

Each soul is distressed.

Each heart is vexed.

Losing near and dear one spills stress,

Crying aloud! For whom the bell tolls next?

Tomorrow and tomorrow and tomorrow

Carona creeps in this petty pace of time.

Will Shakespeare write another sonnet?

Commencing the end of Pandemic chime.

Lockdown has turned poets, musicians, artists and creators,

Teaching people to value time and devote to the Maker.

But Cry my Beloved Country! Cry before God,

Uplift humanity, Be our saviour and shower Benediction.

THE BELLS WERE RINGING EVEN IN THE BIRTH OF LOCKDOWN

A restriction imposed on life is a burden.

Confinement to home is totally cumbersome.

The curb on the hustle and bustle of daily activity all of a sudden,

Raises a question, will the bells be ringing in the lockdown?

An ant creeped out of its hole,

A squirrel scurried past the tree in a roll,

Watching and squirming of these creatures in a flow,

Could not stop wondering, can Pandemic make me feel so low,

Incessantly, hearing the bells ringing even in the birth of lockdown.

A walk in the fields, a smile from a neighbour,

Were actions anchored in a harbour?

Covered faces with masks, peeping eyes, expressionless and cliquish,

Keeping distance, two metres apart, made you apathetic and reclusive,

Misanthropic, unconcerned with the bells ringing in the birth
of lockdown.

A sudden insight into my mind elated my spirits,

Boosting my plight to capture my spirit.

Syllables running riot in the corner of my script,

Framing a backbone of my thoughts with grit,

Will being a poetess permit the ringing of bells in the birth of
lockdown?

Traveling down my memory lane,

I could contemplate the thoughts in reminiscence,

My dream will float through the sea of nescience,

And recall my repressed wishes taking a dip in the ocean,

Emerging triumphant with the bells ringing in the birth of
lockdown.

I felt a fairy dancing to the tune of Mozart's chimes,

A passionate love of nature warbling in lyrical rhymes.

Driving myself crazy in reciting my verses,

Nerve racking, canorous, mellifluous poesies,

The bells NOW ringing in the birth of lockdown.

I lost count of my years with time,

It made me feel young in pandemic prime,

Beauty lay undiscovered in creative envision,

Swerving and blooming with ecstatic vision,

But feeling fortunate with bells still ringing in the birth of lockdown.

PEACE

Peace is a stress-free state of mind, fully pacified,

It tranquilizes and harmonizes the heart and the soul.

It is invisible and transparent,

But yet perceptible and apparent.

Peace is immeasurable.

It has no circumference and dimension,

Which can scale the numbers not mentioned,

Showcasing your scarcity or abundance.

Peace for the poor is having food.

Peace for the rich is having wealth.

Peace for celebrities is having fame.

Peace for an artist is revealing creativity.

Can we equate peace with satisfaction?

Accomplishing fulfillment gives betterment,

Hard labour, toil and perseverance expects rewards,

Appraisal and applause cater to awards.

We strive for success in life,

But length of success fails to measure in scales.

The fever and the fret of the world,

Makes you keep peace remotely forlorn.

You go to school to get education,

College helps you to choose your career,

Profession made you independent,

But peace still looked upon you with a distance.

You are the mistress of the house,

Looked upon your spouse for support,

Searched constant happiness in the children,

But peace still looked upon you with a distance.

You turned benevolent in giving alms to the poor,

You bowed humbly before the wishes of the others,

You were modest in aspiring for good life,

Yet peace smiled at you from a distance.

You prayed to God to shower blessings,

Sat in silence, meditating within,

Searched for happiness within your soul hidden,

Still peace stood ambivalent in the distance.

Fortune is fickle,

Destiny is bitter-sweet,

Fame is vanity,

But Peace is repose in harmony.

Anger, ego, pride all comes before a fall,

Overlooking them strengthens you overall,

Peace is liberty in tranquility,

Which stands with you till eternity.

Personal Poems

RAKSHABANDHAN

Walking down the memory lane,

Reminds me nostalgically how sane,

We were, when as a young dame,

We tied the knots of love without any shame.

Rakhi is a sacred thread without dimension,

Which every year keeps the brother in suspension,

As to what lies in store for him without apprehension,

To emerge on this auspicious day deep in fascination.

Motherhood, Fatherhood, Brotherhood and Sisterhood,

Are family ties that have so strongly stood,

The bonds of relationship upheld by blood,

Whose colour is red but its incessant flow is in flood.

Sisters wait with anxiety,

Brothers work forward with piety,

Mothers are full of compassion worshiping deity,

And of course, fathers pray with all mighty.

Brother, you are an epitome of love,

Among your three sisters, who like dove,

Keep a watch over their humble Lamb they adore,

Who stands with them in all they assure.

Rajeev stands as a signatory white lotus,

Nalini, Pankaj and Neerja are also lotus corniculatus,

Together we splash in vibrant colours of beauty,

Making you emerge as adorable and worthy.

You are a pearl in the Ocean.

Whose soul is as crystal white in constant motion.

In the tepid ebb and flow of life's tide,

You spread your beauty, love and purity with wings wide.

You stand by us, we stand by you,

Unremittingly, unquestionably without raising an eye,

We turn to you; you turn back to us without a big Why?

A saviour in hand, forever a standby.

Richly blessed is how we feel,

Though miles apart keep us sealed.

You are a bright effulgent star,

That we love with all our heart.

Dear brother, keep eternal, these bonds with integrity,

We spread our petals afloat on this sea of life,

Emanating fragrance of love and amicability,

Tying the knots of brotherhood and sisterhood with affability.

TO SIR, WITH LOVE.

Hemendra is the Lord of Gold,

The father and Mother figure so bold,

Your entrepreneurship is marvellous,

Making life far more glamorous.

You won laurels as a teacher,

Professor, Guide and Mentor,

Never availing any advantages,

Standing tall to students' vantage.

You are a Godfather to me,

The epitome of love and friendship.

Closely enlightening what is in your nest,

Outdoing others to do your best.

You stood as a pillar of strength,

Scaling boundaries of perils at every length,

Always firm in your principles of life,

Never yielding to any weakness in each strife.

Your children are the stars that shine,

Bright, courteous, candid and guileless with time.

You have anchored their lives,

Ingenuous and genuine during pitfalls with times.

You are a Saint and a Sage

Who needs no Gita, Bible or Quran to wage,

A Holy war of peace amongst mankind,

Who will gladly trace your footsteps with a cool mind.

A twist in your smile on your face,

Reflects your frank admiration.

A frown on the brow above,

Draws disapproval with a questioning eye.

Your straight and stealthy gait,

Rebuffs the numbers with age.

You are a sturdy hand to hold to,

In times of distress and ache.

You are a source of inspiration,

Being a stalwart of power and grit.

Scaling new heights with age,

Making footprints in life's coon age.

So, you are very special and dear to me.

We bow in reverence to you in obeisance.

We, your children will imbibe your good traits,

Widening our horizons with new dreams and vision.

MY PET

I have two pet dolls, Elsa and Anna,

Do not mistake them as Hannah,

They are dolls who fret and fume,

And dance very much to my tune.

They sit on the sofa, crouched by my side.

Eat while playing hide and seek by bedside,

They relax comfortably on the couch,

And sleep merrily in a pouch.

I laugh, play and run,

Together we have fun.

We ride together on a bike,

And never fail to go on a hike.

Life with parents and pets is full of fun,

Because they teach you to learn and shun,

When I am in a state of stress,

They are my friends to remove my distress.

Sometimes, I find them in a miserable state,

Uncombed, unbathed and undressed,

My duties towards them seem neglected,

But they never complain about this to their mistress.

They are my darlings,

Who stays close to my heart.

Their broad smile and long hair,

Heal my woes which they surreptitiously share.

A BROTHER, MY TREASURE

Brother, you are my treasure,

With 'B', you are the Best,

And 'R' makes you better than the Rest.

So, your collective self-works without any stress.

For our family, you are our heir.

But definitely not invisible like air.

Your presence is felt everywhere,

In each family function and celebration held anywhere.

We siblings are the sum of four.

Three sisters close to you, never forbore,

But turn their eyes to you as our mentor,

Enduring all privations, holding you in the centre.

You are the rootstock of our generation,

To nourish the stems of its filiations,

By being the sire of our fountain,

And the nucleus of our connection.

Your devotion to our parents is unconditional,

Your trifling over minor issues is immaterial.

Your tenderness and warmth towards one and sundry,

Is often commendable and brings appraisal.

The veins of your roots are strikingly clear,

In the soil of your familial peer.

Your branches, Saumitra and Sankalp are meritoriously queer,

Providing nourishment to their twigs, Arjun, Uday and Savi without fear.

These five gems are a treasure to be preserved,

With a mother-queen Sheela, holding the reins unmeasured,

Vibhuti and Sneha, the provenance progenitors

Stand with inspiration to strengthen the foundation of their peers.

My dear Brother, you always stand by my side,

And hold my hand and help me understand.

Your love is like a pearl in the ocean,

That abounds in wealth, surpassing all notions.

SISTERS –UNCONDITIONAL FRIENDS

Sisters, who are you?

A caretaker, mentor, guardian and a mother,

Who multiplies these roles forever,

According to the needs of time altogether.

What is there in a name?

Roses are red and violets are blue,

Nalini and Pankaj are lotuses,

Whose fragrance is sweet, keeping purity in view.

When I was a child, innocent and wild,

Words on paper seemed meaningless and mild.

Learning was an art which was absent with a smile

You both took up the cudgels to teach a sister, then a young child.

Arithmetic was nothing but a jumbled number,

Addition, subtraction, division and multiplication,

Were creating havoc in the mind manifesting complications,

But my sisters, you retrieved my sums like an adventure.

Pale, weak-kneed, anemic was I,

Succumbing to cold, cough and flu was no lie.

Reading rather than retention of letters was to emprise,

You, my sisters, captured my weakness and recouped me with surprise.

Sisters are a teacher, a voracious reader and a creative thinker,

Who encompasses the treasures of learning with zest,

And emerges out as Pollyanna-do-gooder,

An idealist, a visionary, a matriarch and a theorizer.

You are an amalgamation of truth outright,

Lilting the cadences of upheavals upright,

Finding a cure of all illnesses,

Surpassing all my distress with loving caresses.

You both are a replica of my mother

 Abounding in virtues like none other,

Pity, Piety, Patience and Perseverance,

Makes you appease my tantrums with reverence.

I bow in obeisance to you, dear sisters,

You stand by me in all my perils,

Your one thought, one word and concern unveil the secrets,

Opening the doors of understanding discreetly.

WEDDING ANNIVERSARY OF PRITI AND SHOBHIT

Marriage is a conjugation of two souls,

That ties the bonds of lives as a whole.

Time may move and tide may flow,

But togetherness keeps the fervor going.

Twelfth December rings the bells of the great day,

Collecting the flowers which blossom each way,

The opening of each petal from the floweret,

Brings the dawn of each New Year with a sway.

Shobhit and Priti, -Priti and Shobhit,

Mingle together like two love birds.

The canonization of their purity and passion,

Does harmonize the strings of their adulation.

The span of time evokes another image,

Reflected in the birth of their lineage.

Vivaan and Kabir, the two replicas of montage,

Are icons silhouette in family collage.

Love knows no bounds,

But is an analogue which abounds,

With allegiance, fidelity and veneration which rebounds,

By silently exhibiting the variety of its sounds.

May all four of you hem within the perimeter,

Of tenderness and compassion and never deter,

From confines and limitation and restrictions,

Restoring the sweetness of the inner soul with benediction.

Our prayers to the Almighty God,

To see and bless you on your blessed day,

May God always be your companion,

And guide you always on your way.

We wish you marital strength and fortitude,

Holding you both fast and strong amidst fears,

As parents we wish you good health and happiness,

For we know that you will ever be our children whom we adore.

PRITI—PREETY

The vicissitudes of life,

Never end the strife.

Life is not a bed of roses,

But full of problem as doses,

Which act as antidotes of Moses.

Priti, you are the beneficiary,

To peep through with efficacy.

And meet that fiend that lies like truth,

But you overcome it by your tangible fruit

Of knowledge, compassion and delight.

You are the epitome of love and beauty.

Your children cherish you as idol,

And worship you for your fidelity,

Admire you for your loyalty,

Always dote on you for your philanthropy.

Your slenderness, stateliness and stealthiness,

Were the first impressions created indelibly.

Your features reflected your Indian ideals,

Your sweetness enticed our hearts,

Your liveliness invigorated the pinnacles of art.

Your prayers were devotional,

Your love was unconditional,

Your work was admirable,

Your profile was so beautiful.

We cherished to prize you, as soulful.

I love you as my daughter.

Never differentiate you with anyone.

Love, faith, respect, trust, forgiveness,

Is what builds the walls of Home.

I feel blessed to have my two jewels,

Vivaan and Kabir are two gems that dwell,

In this home, shooting their arrows of love from the start.

We embrace them close to our hearts,

May God bestow all his blessings on them.

Even though I might not say so often,

I appreciate all you do.

Your demeanor, your dress, cake and recipes.

Heavenly blessed is how I feel,

Having an elegant daughter, we can perceive.

Reach for the zenith of success,
Because you deserve the best.
You are not just the wife, daughter and mother,
But a woman who comes alive like none other,
You add value to our family by being a treasure.

LOVING DAUGHTER

How do you define a treasure?

Do you have a yardstick to measure?

The dimensions of the soul who is my pleasure,

To have it nearest to my heart with leisure.

Yes, can you fathom the depth of my being?

No scale can delve into the length of seeing,

The heights that she can reach on doing,

The never-ending feats of glory that she is achieving.

Marvelous! You are indeed the mystery of my soul,

That lies buried in the depth of my whole.

Someone whose virtues can never be extolled,

By a mother, father who bears the passion of her every

role.

My daughter, Shobhna, who trudges the path with grit and

determination,

Who breaks the shackles of life with love and resolution.

She is none other but a true replica of her parents,

And breathes the aroma of strength into her origin.

I look up to her and visualize my past, present and future,
with conviction.
No matter whatever and wherever I will be,
You will be there to hold my hand with love and
compassion,
Because you are the quintessence of Everything that God
blessed me with,
I bow in deep obeisance to Him for this.

LOVING SON

Thunderstorm and lightning,

Played havoc in nature.

Black clouds created a dread,

Of torrential downpours with a threat.

Rivers were overflowing,

Casting a spell over oceans,

Breaking bars of bondage in jail,

Lord Krishna was born.

Similar were the circumstances,

That gave birth to a humane soul,

A divinity of my heart,

Who I cherish as our offspring is so smart.

A child who bore the brunt of nature,

Cuddled and nestled in the lap of a mother.

Possessing virtues of love and gentleness,

Being an apple of my eye with tenderness.

Tall and stately

Healthy and wise,

Persevering and devoted,

In reaching the goals of his life.

Your playfulness and pranks,

Enraptured us in a trance,

Sticking to his principles with austerity,

Being determined to soar high in eternity.

You graduated and mastered,

In the field of engineering,

Never wavering from your path,

Being bold, unnerved in every art.

You left your roots in India,

Flying high to the States with zest.

Being reverential and compassionate,

With your spouse as your mate.

Your devotion to parents,

Can never be questioned.

Standing the trials of life,

With faith and conviction.

You are a blessed father,

To your two jewels in life,

Cherishing and nurturing them,

In every walk of life with might.

Our prayers to Lord Krishna as our saviour,

Who blessed our heavenly abode.

Feeling enamoured and entranced,

Living my dreams with a son, a facsimile of our life.

www.ingramcontent.com/pod-product-compliance
Lightning Source LLC
Chambersburg PA
CBHW022001150726
47990CB00002B/554